Enormous Ears

and Soft Brown Hair

Whose Little Baby Are You?

by Ellen Lawrence

Ruby Tuesday Books

Published in 2016 by Ruby Tuesday Books Ltd.

Editor: Mark J. Sachner
Designer: Emma Randall
Production: John Lingham

Photo Credits:
Alamy: 7, 10–11; Cosmographics: 23 (top); FLPA: 12–13,
15, 16–17; Anders Lindgren: 6; Public Domain: 22 (top);
Shutterstock: Cover, 1, 4–5, 8–9, 14, 16 (top), 18–19, 20–21,
23 (bottom).

Library of Congress Control Number: 2015940228

ISBN 978-1-910549-18-6

Printed and published in the United States of America

For further information including rights and
permissions requests, please contact our Customer
Service Department at 877-337-8577.

Contents

Words shown in **bold** in the text are explained in the glossary.

A New Baby in the Forest

Forest

Among the trees in a forest, there lives a baby animal.

The baby has enormous ears and a coat of soft brown hair.

Who does this little baby belong to?

Mother moose

Newborn calf

6

The baby, or calf, belongs to a mother moose.

The little calf was born on a sunny spring morning.

His mother gently licked him clean.

By the afternoon, the calf was able to stand.

At first, the calf's long, thin legs were a little wobbly.

By the end of his first day, however, the baby moose could walk.

A one-day-old moose calf

A one-week-old moose calf

Within a few days, he could run—fast!

The calf stays close to his mother at all times.

The mother moose keeps watch for bears and wolves that might hurt her baby.

If a **predator** comes close, she kicks it with her large hooves.

Moose calf

Mother moose

A calf
drinking milk

The calf drinks milk from his mother.

Sometimes, he drinks standing up.

Sometimes, the calf and his mother
sit down when it's time to feed.

The mother moose eats plants.

She munches on leaves, new shoots, twigs, and tree bark.

Mother moose

When he is about
two weeks old,
the calf tries this
grown-up food.

A two-week-old
moose calf

15

The mother moose also likes to eat water plants that grow in lakes and streams.

A six-month-old moose calf

When mom wades into a lake, the calf goes, too.

As the summer passes by, the calf grows bigger and stronger.

Mother moose

When he is about one year old, the calf is ready to live alone and take care of himself.

Soon, bony **antlers** start to grow from his head.

Antlers

The antlers grow and grow.

Antlers

When he is six years old, the moose is all grown up.

Now he has enormous antlers.

He weighs more than 1,000 pounds (454 kg).

He has become a tall, powerful adult bull moose.

An adult bull moose

Fact File

All About Moose

Moose are the largest members of the deer family. They are also known as elk.

Only male moose grow antlers.

Moose are fast runners and strong swimmers.

Each year, a moose's antlers fall off in winter. Then a new pair grows in spring.

A moose's antlers can measure 6 feet (1.8 m) from tip to tip.

Moose Size

Male moose

Female moose

Man   Woman

Moose Weight

Adult male:
Up to 1,600 pounds (726 kg)

Adult female:
Up to 900 pounds (408 kg)

Newborn calf:
30 pounds (14 kg)

Where Do Moose Live?

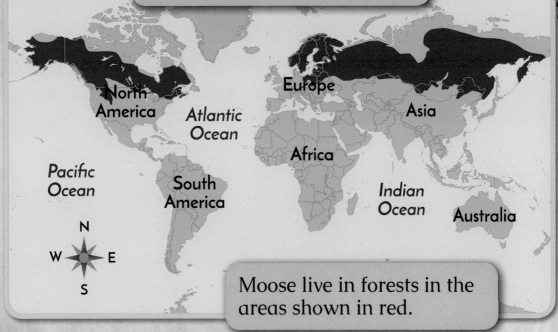

North America

Europe

Asia

Atlantic Ocean

Africa

Pacific Ocean

South America

Indian Ocean

Australia

N W E S

Moose live in forests in the areas shown in red.

Moose Moms and Dads

Adult moose live alone. Males and females meet up when it's time to **mate**.

A mother moose and calf

A female moose is ready to have a baby when she's about two years old.

Sometimes a female moose gives birth to twin calves.

Father moose do not help take care of their calves.

Glossary

antlers (ANT-lurz)
Large, branchlike body parts made from bone that grow from a deer's head.

mate (MATE)
To get together to have babies.

predator (PRED-uh-tur)
An animal that hunts and eats other animals.

Index

antlers 18–19, 20, 22

food 12–13, 14–15, 16

forests 4, 23

male (bull) moose 20–21, 22–23

mother moose 6–7, 10–11, 12–13, 14, 16–17, 23

predators 10

running 9, 22

Read More

Hemstock, Annie. *Moose (Pebble Plus)*. Mankato, MN: Capstone Press (2012).

Owen, Ruth. *Moose (Dr. Bob's Amazing World of Animals)*. New York: Rosen Publishing (2014).

Learn More Online

To learn more about moose, go to
www.rubytuesdaybooks.com/whoselittlebaby